Hanging Fire

Phyllis Webb

Hanging Fire

Coach House Press · Toronto

Some of the poems have previously appeared in the
following magazines and anthologies: *The Malahat
Review, Grain, Prairie Fire, The Massachusetts
Review, Canadian Literature, Zymergy, Somewhere
Across the Border, Open Letter, The Capilano Review,*
and *The Second Macmillan Anthology*
(eds. John Metcalf and Leon Rooke).
'Messages' first appeared in my book *Talking*,
Quadrant Editions, Montreal, 1982.

The quotation from 'musing with mothertongue' by
Daphne Marlatt may be found in *Touch to My Tongue*,
Longspoon Press, Edmonton, 1984, p. 45.

Grateful thanks, once again, to the Canada Council
for a Senior Arts Award in 1987.

Canadian Cataloguing in Publication Data

Webb, Phyllis, 1927-
Hanging fire

Poems.

ISBN 0-88910-391-7

I. Title.

PS8545.E22H3 1990   C811'.54   C90-094785-3
PR9199.3.W43H3 1990

In memory of the poets

Gwendolyn MacEwen, bpNichol,
Bronwen Wallace

in poetry ... sound will initiate thought by a process of association. words call each other up, evoke each other, provoke each other, nudge each other into utterance ... a form of thought that is not rational but erotic because it works by attraction. a drawing, a pulling toward, a 'liking.'

Daphne Marlatt
musing with mothertongue

Titles of poems in quotation marks are 'given' words, phrases, or sentences that arrive unbidden in my head. I've been tracking them for some time to see if there are hidden themes, connections, a sub-rational rationale. It seems there are.

P.W.

Contents

Scattered Effects

Tour de Force

'A Model of the Universe'

The arrogance. The above it all.
Ministrations of angels,
little holy ghosts fiddling
while the planets burn, sing.
For instance, superstrings,
immense smallness of, tangled
spaghetti, the metaphor
materializing unimaginable
piquant sauce, restores us
to middling size, for comparison:
minute white floss on the rose-
mary plant, one flower in bloom
of Queen Anne's lace.

Or shady dealings in the lab.
A hand-made mouse with cancer
for generations, patented,
marketed, sold, as transgenetic
engineering steers us to the
unity of all things.

I put my foot down on
such nonsense, trinkets of ever-
lasting gloom, animal suffering.
If I tangle with invisible
superstrings, hung up on
supergravity, elegant
mathematics, all this
weighty knowledge ...

'Krakatoa' and 'Spiritual Storm'

Hot magma
        indigo dawn
wild yelps
        of pure physics
crack open deep sea
buttocks thrust up love lava
world heart / broken / cardiac
arrest.
Krakatoa. Krakatau.

The small gods gather
for countdown, each lifts
a finger to the wind (quake,
tide, tsunami) tastes
the cost of all-paroxysmal
sexual storm, lid blown off,
creator creating, a whim,
wham of blowup on shores –
Java, Sumatra, Hawaii –
blasting away 2200 miles heard,
Krakatoan wind circling the dust
up high enough. Radiant

marvellous sunsets for years.
Spectacle. Le monocle de mon
oncle sent flying into the eye
of the storm (*spiritual* for him,
timbre just right, *pinhead*).

God how I suffer to get this down as if I'd
been there watching the lava hit and run after
dogs and children and hens, cone island collapsing
into the sea. Always this me. Tourist, back-packed,
camera at ready, lens cap removed.

And the big gods come, finally, to the Pacific
for 36,000 dead, fallout, cinders, oracular
birth of Anak (child of) Krakatoa. Bad mouth.
Ash. Devolution. Darkness at noon.

So be it. So it was: May 20, 1883, 'paroxysmal'
blast August 26, 'climax' eruption August 27,
10 a.m. Masses of floating pumice near the
volcano so thick as to halt ships. Surrounding
region in darkness two and a half days.
Temperature world-wide lowered 0.27°.
Plant and animal life gone five years.
Anak (child of) Krakatoa active into
the 1980's.

Genetic spleen

Time lapse backwards

Mortal fear
Cassandra
Nostradamus
'Sons of guns'

I cannot surprise you. Not with the blue jay's
return. Not with the velvet yellow of pansyface,
not with my held-back fire. Apocalypse. Every-
thing predictable in the book. Ominous ocean.
Glacier waterslide. Occult fecal blood's old
testament. Rotted bodies. Sun's eclipse.
Venus swinging below the moon.

Veracity. Storm, calm, dilemmas, ditch-jumps.
Capacity for wonder. The spring of the mouse-
trap sprung, we are caught – thus and so – in
this pose, shadowed beyond doubt. Fire hanging
back for a more effective, filmic test-site,
for desert bloom.

for Dorothy Livesay and bill bissett

'Miasma'

Stunned by the blow
          polluting exhalations
poisonous effluvium
(infectious, noxious) putrid
matter and such a lovely
sound/word I hear 'mimosa'
hidden there, the daze
the out-and-out sunshine yellow
of delirium, fever, malarial
swamp-garden.
How the mind doth know
its own dictionary. Ditch-
water/standing-water
still reflecting a bullrush,
calf, dragonfly, echo of
plasma, old hoe-down
razzmatazz of this affliction.
Gear-lock, warlock,
critter of the moon.

'Sliding Doors'

Between rosy dawn and the fifth dimension, the Morning Star shrugs and staggers off stage-right. But the flight's on time, sparks spackle the skyway with interludes of starling song. Trills, *pianissimo,* thunder above, Crimean surgery explores the lower gut, salvation at the edge of a blade, a summer of Sundays. Hah. One foot's through a place called EXIT, the other aboard sky-surfing nebulae. Vasty undertakings. God-awful daily grind.

'The Mind of the Poet'

Slippages, repeat performance, soundings profounder as down we go for the third time through green waters, pearl-diving, operatic; or dead poets brought back on their knees second time around, gartersnakes splitting through mind-burn, matter-disorders. Ho Hum. Jumping bugs. What a parade of fancy-frees, scared shitless half the time, sorrowing saints, dumb pets waiting for the can to open. *Bird brains, eagle eyes, sad sacks,* whose minds float on forgetfulness – to quartz, sapphire, topaz, emerald-hard memory shards, spooky auditions, Toad of Toad Hall greeting his guests at the door with his white butler's gloves on.

'Eidetic Image'

Blasé, having seen it all before blaze forth, 'shook foil' or fingerprint, a big toe pronged, little one cracked on a hub. Whimsy, shenanigans, Irish clowns, Irish poets mad, like me, murderous Othellos, Pagliaccis. Oh, I would sing if I had a mind to, but I don't have the heart in images' aftersnow, in 'in memoriams'. Istanbul's still a thong away, but in that Paris café the waiter came hungry for kisses. Garçon!

Objects from the past   eye-patch   or   eye catch mesmerism   tick-tock of waitings   arrivals so-longs   too many rushes of Pennsylvania (where she's never been) Pilgrim Fathers sad in their black brigades   the old found land   the far countree

'Seeking Shape. Seeking Meaning'

Hot pursuit, or languorous. We are in. A blue lagoon
bird stands on one pale leg, a picture of reflection,
nothing ruffled. Waters lap, ingenious insects walk
on water; thoughts bloom like algae, fluorescent,
many-celled, liberated and dying in their own element.

* * *

The syntax of deep structure composes on the harp,
strings along.

* * *

Red hot spikes. Fire-walking.

* * *

Cadence in scene, in the *seen*, seeking out pattern,
finding where the eye catches, heart hooks, tangible
order, a cadence. Tantrums of tears at such pure
spirit, radiant things, on which the eyes close.

* * *

'Mind is shapely, Art is shapely.' Ginsbergian insight,
Allen afloat on his untidy chaos, his good humours. Ahoy!

* * *

Fragmentation: to understand the parts, reify certain
curious particulars to our habit of framing.
(Management techniques – precious jewels in the Swiss
          watch,
the Cretacious period slotted between Jurassic and
Cenozoic. See chart under GEOLOGY. See geology under
the chart.

* * *

Some of it makes sense, shape, meaning meandering river of biologic 'soup' on which fish, birds, insects feed, that feed us. River on which we move undulant, forsaking all else for this infectious cruise.

'Cornflowers & Saffron Robes
Belittle the Effort'

Ssh, sigh, silence is coming, the night time blues. Hark.
Ahem. Sir? I lift my arm, the wind chimes through my
holy raiment. Mesmeric bells reduce the flies to slum-
ber. Pajama party. The end of the Raj.

'Self City'

Tram tracks, Metro, torso
junction; gunshots, expectorations,
bird twitter; eternal castle
on the hill,
passages, narrow, through
the problematics.

I speak, therefore I am,
or so I say, seeing
the egoless Transcendent
poised on the parapet,
armed & dangerous.

Bed-sitter, rock-bottom,
urban clutter.
Words. Words
jumping the gun
on soundlessness.
The river flows on,
of course, vile stream
of ever-exchanging platitudes.

'As Rare as Hens' Teeth'

a needle in a haystack
as rare as hens' teeth
a nose for news pushing
the fallen leaves back
for luscious worms
composted cash. Ai! Ai!
I've fallen over again
into *despond*, occluded
rage. I tear up another
page of pilgrim's progress
I lie on Donne's love's
violet bank, say nothing
all the day, nothing into
the cliché-ridden night.
Pray you, undo this button.
Show me one hen's tooth.
I'll find the needle.
Thread it.

'Temporal Lobe'

Migraine, on the sinistral,
right brain hammering left.
Bad science. Bad faith.
It's been a long time,
one outgrows them, they say.
But today.
Writhings, rage clenches
my fist. Frozen pea-bag
smashes against the hearth.
Tears on the crocodile
pillow. Housebound.
Inwardbound. Pacing.
The wall-to-wall carpet
raises its ugly head
accosts my dead languages.
Wait for the pills to take:
heightened consciousness,
intense forms. Purple iris
astonishing after rain,
June greens green, greener.
My face? It too articulates
each muscle into word-spasms,
syllable kicks. Three poems
in one day. Breathing fire.
Swallowing hard. Arrogant
sentence fragments. *Can't
get out.*

'Compendium'

The weight of the world, Atlas,
or you, whoever you are, it's
the way our lives hang in the
balance, it's two-for-the-price-
of-one, Mao's Little Red Book,
the Home Hardware flyer, it's
frozen tears stashed on the
bathroom shelf.
Hanging together, we speak
volumes. Spoke.

'Gate Crashing'

Flutter of eyelash, mirror of rabbit's sick eyes. Experimental pain, gate-lock on all that expression. Exploring the good old times, mascara, seduction, sex-ploys. What you have to know is the technical procedure: implantation of dyes, location of cornea. *Loco. Loco.* The cries of the animals for 'human interest' in my friend's continuing pain – his hearing those cries in the worst nights, his blessing of the animals, two by two.

'The Mills of God'

That flying Dutchman's caught on his own windmill,
puffs himself up with genuine ether laughter. Around
and about wind plays tricks and suddens, scoops a paw
into the local topsoil, nothing here, nothing to do, alas.

'The Salt Tax'

SATYA-GRA-HA. SATYA-GRA-HA. I never saw the MOO-VEE- VEE-VEE-VEE or the OP-OP-OP-PRAH (by Philip Glass) and at the age of three I could not, in 1930, have grasped the meaning of the salt tax-ax-ax-ax, but might have seen a pho-oh-toe of Gandhi in the newspaper (and the power of TROOTH, as children do), of the skinny old ma-ahn and his 78 followers trickling down 200 miles to the edge of the Arabian Sea at Dandi on the entrance to the Gulf of Cambay.

Today and yesterday and the day before, the sliding doors opened to let me (age 61) see him (age 61) again as a vision of sparse white cloth, and hear-ear-ear again 'child's play', which is what he said walking 10 or 12 miles a day had been all the way from Ahmedabad.

Satya-gra-ha-ha-ha, he had written before the trek, seriously to Lord Irwin, 'Take your own salary. It is over 21,000 ru-ooh-pees per month ... you are getting over 700 ru-ooh-ooh-pees a day, against India's average income of less than 7 annas [4 cents] per day (eh-eh-eh?). Thus you are getting over 5,000 times India's average in-come-come-come! On bended knee, I ask you to ponder over this phe-nom--e-non-non ...'

On bended knee? And they walked on over the strewn petals, the strewn leaves, cheered by many villagers, the salt of the earth-earth-earth, on-on

to the Arabian ocean's taste of tears, sah-ah-tya- yah-yah-gra-ha-ha-ah – ah, beautiful grace as they bent down to steal a handful of free-ee-dom.

'You Have My Approval'

Well, thank *you* very much. The indices prick up their ears, they tabulate the prospects – quick, a hit of doctrine. The poem expands its chest, looks you straight in the eye, knows you for who you pretend to be, says, The game is up, Buster, let's get serious.

Instructions for the faint of heart

Turn the turtle over. Test its white stomach.
Find your island. Find the treasure.
Take short naps through the heat of the day.
Drink clean water only, if you can find it.
Build a wall – or not at all.
Lead your pretty shadow by the pretty hand.

Terrorist directives

Know the code.
Translate it into a foreign language. Any foreign language.

Memorize the Plan. Do not try to understand it.
Make a new plan. Make a list. A longer list.
Forget it.

Crash course in Chaos science; likewise Particle Physics.

Abscond with the Access to Information Act.
Advertise your whereabouts on national TV.

Call the hot-line. Say you're on your way with a crack death squad.

Say your Now-I-lay-me's.

Have a drink on me.

'The Way of All Flesh'

flash – at the corner of the eye
(right corner, right eye). The car
has crashed at the bottom of the hill;
its motor purrs like a sick cat,
and you read this as contentment.

Hanging Fire

'Hanging Fire'

Furioso, flame-eyed Flamenco, castanets' death
rattle.

Guru from the frozen North heats up shamanically,
her two big feet *Southbound.*

As lights go out, crisis of lambency.

'Dresden/China' – or thereabouts.

A curtain of fire drops over the overview,
glass-like substances, 'fragments of quartz'.

They leap and hang in the air. Firebugs.
Organic memory goes up in smoke.

Action. Smiling. Acidulous. Eating its heart out.

'Ignis Fatuus'

Sunlight sprays through rain; wind tumbles surf,
globe of a morning moon glows down – here, where
we need all the light we can get.

* * *

As if by design, nets fail. Shellfish pinch the
bottom of the bay. Floods of power. Surges of
information.

* * *

'Manitou'

* * *

Alders, elders, birch trees on the road to
Moscow's airport.

* * *

Down at the beach at night, we poked the sea
with sticks, stirred up the .*.

night-blooming phosphorous.

* * *

Ignis fatuus, foolish fire, jack-o'-lantern, will-
o'-the-wisp. Marsh light from decomposing matter.
Delusional systems. Us.

* * *

'The Unbearable Lightness ...'

Heavyweight a
heavy wait for
that unbearable that
moment of being
a featherweight a
spin of spume
on a dark wave a
wave of the hand's
farewell into
freefold
mystical fire's
wild mandala –
orange and gold
amoeba-like edges
breathing and push-
ing in weight-
less and out
on wall (spurge
mustard seed
primula) violent
centre-spawn
marauding the doubt-
less dust-filled
last gasp
unbearable morning
light being
switchable on and

'You Are Nowhere'

in the work. The work is kin.
It's all in the family.

The old brain beats: Opera, Opus,
opulent film of disease, disaster

opening, closing on the one hand and
on the other, the jewels of dualism.

You are somewhere in the world
of 'the fire next time'.

I am trying to find you.
You are nowhere. Somewhere

in the spas of Romanian cures,
Islamic solutions –

or into a slow fade of alpha waves,
floats of lepidoptera –

for Salman Rushdie

hanging f   hanging f   hanging f   hanging f
    ire   ire   ire   ire

```
hanging f
          ear
    hanging f
              ear
    hanging f
              ear
hanging f
      ear
```

"LENIN SKATING"

PATiN A patiner   theSTARS
         PATINA   patiner   patina   under
                                               theSTARS
                                                 the

         MoonLightIce

     tHE TSARS

              at 15YEA
                  Sr

                heskates

ON THE FROZen volGA
      on the froZen Volga THE FROZEN VOLGA

         AT SIMBIRSk
                    SI
                 SR thebladescutcleanthrough
    ERO CI   ER
       O   the
                      fu tur E
                              er ose ro ser
       ballet
              i chisfigures 888888ssss
    THE TSARS*
              *
               *
                *
                 *
                  **** * Ω ΩΩ Ω Δ
                     ***** Ω Ω Ω
                    *   Δ   μμμμμμμμμμμ
    VLADIMIRVLADIMIR *   >>>>>>>> <<<<<<<<
                          θθ
                          θθ θθθθθθθθ
    <<<<<<<<<<<<<<<<<<<<<<<<<<<<<<<<<<< θ θθθθθθθθ>

```
s*
 n o*                "M O T H            R U S S I A"              *   *
f* we                    a n o t                                      *
 l*                         h er r us s i a  viborg              %*%
a k *s*        at the FIN LAND Station                              D N
        *      [April 3 (old style)1917]        PETERSBURG         U O
                                                                 O S
   his  cOmrade      revolutionrevolutionrevolu        MARX
      wife  leninsays lenin...                              S
 NADYA       (taking notes)                         SP*  A
  (taking notes)                                         A R K

  the PEOPLE        PEACE              WORLD
    e PEOPLE            sash a          history
 NEED PEACE                        olga        le n i
                                   motheranna      n sa ys
  th e                           AND THEY GIVE
  PEOPLE                          you W A R &&&
 NEEDBREAD                           HUNGER!
    etc.
 HURRAH!     HURRAH!                          S
 S T A R* IK                        HURRAH!
       "stari k"                   the P A T R i  H C
 W                                  I               a r
 h     againstdescriptionagainstde  N
 i   vladimirilyi ch uLanovo         E    comrade
 t                          y         s     sailors
 e   'the masses'                  h    A   UNITE
     QQQQQQQQQQQQ  Q   Q    o  o    e    A his com ra de
     QQQQQQQQQQetc.  Q              r way to     mistress
        QQQQQQQQQQQQQQ                    TO M
        QQQQQQQQQQQQQ                   SC O w
              etc.
```

'To the Finland Station'

June 25, 1989. Helsinki train station. I buy Kleenex, oranges, and The Guardian for the trip. I'm missing Bill and Tiff more now that the conference is over. This was to be the special 'non-literary' part of the journey. But it's good to rest, be quiet after all that talk. I'm haunted by Lenin's ghost, the image of the sealed train. Why this obsession? The Romance of Revolution? The last agony of the Oedipus complex? The anxiety of (patriarchal) influence? The poem's pure, peculiar means and ends.

Gorky parked around the station seeing suspicious characters everywhere, then boarded the train. My new Finnish friends told me to head straight for the dining-car for caviar and vodka. But nyet. No caviar, no vodka, no sole almandine today. I watch as the train pulls past unmoving box-cars sprayed solid and lurid with grafitti, but what the words say I don't know. The countryside's sparse and lovely. I try to see it with Lenin's slanty eyes, blinking. Did it look very different in April, 1917?

At the border, armed guards on the parapet. A long stop on both sides. I get my rubles, study the Russian alphabet, want to talk to the Japanese travellers, don't want to talk to anyone. Will the *Intourist* greeter be there at the station? Of course, and I'm hurried into a car and taken to the Moskva Hotel. It's all too speedy. I can't catch up with that old movie in my head.

Up Nevsky Prospekt in the just past midsummer night, feeling low. Everything dusty and crumbly in the heat wave. 'I think, the poetry is/not the words.' Barry McKinnon. He meant, I think, the melody lingers on. In *The Death of a Lyric Poet*. I turn back, it's too late.

June 26. Spectacular entrance into the dining-room this morning – I slipped and fell with force, but no serious damage, except to my self-confidence. Touristy stuff today. Long walk exploring in the a.m., then the usual delays and hurdles to get the bus to Petrodvorets on the Gulf of Finland. Peter the Great's getaway, 'Mon Plaisir'. It is, it is. Inside jammed with sightseers, outside hot, easy, wild grasses, flowers, a trick fountain where kids and grown-ups play.

I still don't understand what was the inspiration to restore these old palaces and mansions of the aristocracy. Was it a prophetic vision of the tourism industry? Or the deep down conservateur instinct? Post-war delusions of grandeur, or make-work? There's more to it than just (just!) the 'People's palaces'.

I've planned to meet R. outside the hotel (Soviet citizens are not supposed to enter these tourist domains). I'd sent a photo so he recognizes me, we take a cab, he insists on paying. As we enter the scruffy elevator in the high-rise, he calls the building a slum, the beginning of the revelations of their unhappiness. I tell him it could be Toronto or New York. A real Russian welcome, even a big cake. I've brought a few gifts – CDs, a book on UFOs, pantihose for L. And vodka. R. demonstrates his superb sound system, too loud for me. They complain about shortages, everything's worse, their disillusionment. Their son wants to be a drummer in a jazz band, says he hates anti-semites, repeats passionately he hates anti-semites, he's 'one-quarter' Jewish, they still want out.

We watch a popular satiric TV news program during which (R. translates) the day's haul at the jail is reviewed. A young man has been arrested because he did a take-off in a public place of the famous Lenin pose: one arm out in orating fashion, one hand tucked into the vest, as in the statue at the Finland Station. When asked by the interviewer why he did it, for the hell of it, he says. The power of parody. I forgot to ask if he also did the speech, 'The people need bread ...'

I love the ride through the Leningrad night in the taxi, elated by my visit to their home. This would not have been possible in 1967 when we first met. Contingency.

June 27. The Hermitage today where I lose my tour group at just the right moment – on my way to the Impressionist collection. Then, later, I have to hurry to find my way back to the bus, parked on the far side of the huge square. Flashes of Tienanmen, flashes of here, the Tsars' old palace guards, the troops, the 'clashes'.

In the evening I have a drink, new to me, Bitter Cinzano, at the hotel bar with a woman cellist from the U.S. She talks a lot about her jewels. It's still light, so we take a stroll in the park-cemetery across the way. Poets' graves with real and plastic flowers, some old dusty downand-outers, and young guys trying to do a blackmarket currency deal. Can't get a line by Odysseas Elytis out of my head: 'All of us with eaten faces will return some day from the Truth-sites.'

Tomorrow – back to the Hermitage, back to Helsinki, back to the Finland Station.

'Passacaglia'

The poet dives off the deep end
of the lyric poem to surface on
Nevsky Prospekt in Leningrad
on a hot June night
missing her friends who ought
to be here in the hot night
walking up Nevsky Prospekt
she has broken her habit of
repetition, the snowdrops,
the snowdrops, the snowdrops
in the white nights, white
nights, white nights, the
death of the lyric poem
the death –

'Long Suffering'

Long suffering is active, alive with plenipotentiaries of
the dead and gone, the lingering on of the living, long
strolling afternoons of carry-me-forward to darkness.
But first the sun goes dawn in plumes. Come. The
hand-in-hand – *a failure of will, a stumbling* –

* * *

Say it again, 'The Years', the art of fiction, the art of
pleasing, pleasures of pain. Or HEAD-ON: strike, revolu-
tion, power overthrown and not overthrown. Burned out
of her home again, she carries the flame. Oppressive
regime. Corruption. Gorge rises on clips of language,
clips of film. No news is bad news. Those who lie slain.

* * *

Tame my heart, featherbrain, you who are not tamed
squawk and feed your young, and then you leave them
hungry to flop up the cedar bough, sway, test wormy
freedom with a lift of small wings. That nature is a dia-
lectical fire. That nature is

* * *

Long-suffering.

* * *

These moths, white, float in and out of Douglas fir, tribal
simples, grazing.

* * *

'The pleasure of the text'. I treat myself to lunch at the
pub, sip cool gazpacho, snatch at 'a poem about terror',
leave when the noise level gets too high.

* * *

The pools of the damned reflect a blood-stained eye, it stares, bulls-eye, I say, on target, as usual.

* * *

A dart-board at the pub jabbed and jabbed again. Rules of the game. Class, analysis. The old Dad's Cookies factory where I first read Marx: friable proportions – or that's the way the cookie crumbles. Dearie.

* * *

I practice tangential existence – necessity, economy, art, use. Big words, small world, bombarded by particle physicists – and butterflies whose effects are infinite.

* * *

Musical interlude. Tralalala-la. I pack my things. Largo doloroso. Adagio for strings. I strangle a scream in the wrong key. The little fish jump up, nevertheless, scales shining. Stravinsky's firebird sings in the heavenly shade-tree, *con fuoco.*

Scattered Effects

'Ambrosia'

Bee-sweet, the honey now/how trails a star
of far/near hawthorn and roseate late leap year

Gerard Manley, your black cassock
rushing through cosmic and microcosmic

inscaped latitudes. I look, see you
passing away/through Jesuitical

raced time-future. All your musculature
stretched, taut, reaching out/off

from black clouds, momentary passage,
there to here, tears of *your* Christ

mix/mingle 'I am so happy, so happy',
your last wet watering words,

June the 8th's hawthorn-hoped, pied beauties,
beatitudes, 1889, heard

here, February, leapings of '88,
10.15 a.m. The 24th.

'Evensong'
(even song syllabics)

Tending toward music, the artist's
life tends toward solitary notes, slips
of the tongue, hand, eye, eerily like
intelligence of higher orders.
Hierarchical systems of dream
stuff, choirs of angelic lisps, minty
panpipes accompanying dawn, mist
rising from hills, green-splits, gold flecks, flicks
of day ascending. No one goes home.
They're out and about, lured by goat god
music-food into noon sun hot rays,
bothered, skewered on oily spit, fat
and famished; one note more, another
tugs them into laid-back afternoon,
lawlessness. Wine, sun sets their steps on
cool path's mythic return, labouring
all the way home. Quiet entrances,
doffed hats, feet on wood, stone, a chair, and
evensong's slim, uncanny sibilance.

'Anaximander'
610-546? BC

Nectar, attar of roses, gardenias gaze from the shade. Anaximander sits on a rock inventing the patient sundial. He sits on a rock in the Greek style, bathed in primary matter, puzzled, at home in his puzzlement, the grand motions of the universe, his minutes slipping away.

* * *

For me, too, it was garden, that day the rufous hummingbird bounced in the spray of the hose as I watered the roses. Inspired – roses, hummingbird, and me – precisely because of the boredom of how things are, and nectar.

* * *

The Grand Unified Theory. A crystal ballroom lined with mirrors. Reflection. To be whole, seen from all sides at once, make sense.

* * *

Gold watch on my wrist, gold sun on the land, movement and shadows. Milesian godfather, cartographer as well as why not everything?

* * *

Yes. No. Two words are better than one during the paradigm shift. Spit and hold your finger to the wind. Which way is blowing? Is blowing the lid off your head? Is prose. Poem?

* * *

Dr. Melzack applies electrodes to the lab cat's brain. I want to die. I want to die again. The good doctor, they say, they say, for your own good.

* * *

53

I sit on a rock in the wood and study the mosses. The bosses of philosophy pace up and down, auras of fanatic gold pulsing around them.

* * *

I tap my own temple. It taps back an undeciphered code, an ode to spring, perhaps, to the skylark, nightingale, pleased with its own whistling.

* * *

Rose-colored glasses, a shift in the mood, or indigo, odd angles, surfaces like mica, cosmos and microcosmos, glazed and changing.

* * *

His One substance. Opposing powers. Those silly wheels of fire, the planets orbiting.

for Smaro Kamboureli

'Attend'

Between 'attached' and 'aloft'
getting the poem on the page
a voice tells her on this day
attend.
Harrowed she is, anguished
by this day's dailiness
teenaged son in danger
following forwardness
as the poem records Bach
in invisible margins, neighbour
pruning his shrubs, her baby-
sitter sorting out her own love-
life at Bino's Pancake House.

This is the way the world –
this is the way I pick up on
the voice in my head today
offering 'valium', substance
long gone, used up in my last
big job and love affair,
its breakdown. *Velvet,* it leads
me on, vole, variorum, text to –
– *stumbling block,* unblocked
and falling over myself in files,
folios, fricatives, freesias – ah
freesias, the scent, spring, sickness,
planting now in Fall my hyacinths –
you brought me hyacinths – and Edith
Sitwellian rain, bombs falling
on London, that old poverty.

So I go, so she
sits at her desk, attending.
To wedding plans, Matisse in the

offing, possible poems
feared and held off for a moment
in her new life, or old one
revised, rough-drafted in the
coil of my cigarette smoke, my next
word being 'lavender'. Lavender
Allen, childhood friend, far back,
Victorian Lavender's innocence
gone surely by now, my own
purple's vengeance, as Bach
counterpoints his clear-eyed
fingering of her poems and mine,
the freeplay, the scandal
murmuring in shrubs this strange
infinitive (listen, I can't believe
it) – *to frolic.*

for Sharon Thesen

'There *Are* the Poems'

An editor asks me to put it all down: the reasons I write.
And I thought 'it' was a gift. Homo ludens at play among
the killing fields of dry grasses. Playful woman making a
space to breathe. 'There *are* the poems,' Sharon says, she
means, between the critical flash. There *are* the poems,
like fists wearing birthstones and bracelets, her 'roses &
bliss'. Or they're like legs running, bounding over the
fields of force, momentum, for a quick roll in Darwin's
tangled bank. And there are the poets doing what? And
why, the editor asks. What does he want? Contributions
to knowledge? Civilisation and its discontents? Chaos
among the order – or, oh yes, french doors opening onto a
deck and a small pool where we can watch our weird
reflections shimmering and insubstantial? The proper
response to a poem is another poem. We burrow into the
paper to court in secret the life of plants, the shifty
moon's space-walks, the bliss, the roses, the glamorous
national debt. Someone to talk to, for God's sake, some-
thing to love that will never hit back.

'Pepper Tree'

The pepper tree opens its arms
to the fifth of March
it greets the fog
and rabbits springing
across a heath
somewhere in Scotland.
It believes in Henry Miller
and that other bastard Picasso.
It believes in its own genius,
suddenly, after winter.
It shines with land claims.
It turns with the hidden sun
praising Winnie Mandela
and Nelson
and Cory Aquino
it roots itself
down into this small-minded pot of darkness
and – *illico* – spins out into
the whirlwind.
It finds ecstatic form by changing places.
It changes places.

Messages

'They are always projecting themselves.
Cats play to cats we cannot see.
This is confidential.'
(Letter from E.D. Blodgett)

The young psychic comes back from halfway down the hall
to tell me to write about the cat on the postcard
tacked to the wall above my typewriter.
There is an understanding between us, and I show her
a photo in the *Journal* where the cat appears behind
my shoulder –

A piece of politics. A creature of state.

Out of Ptolemy's reign, cast in bronze (earrings restored)
far from Egypt now in its northern home.
Probable use: to hold the bones of a kitten.
Representative on this earth of the Goddess Bastet.

She prances toward me down the ramp of the poem
sent to me by the young psychic who is writing
an historical novel.
She moves toward me through an aura composed
of new light and the golden dust of Ptolemy.
Halfway down the ramp her high ears turn against
the task of the poem toward allurements
of stockmarket and monopoly.

Cats play to cats we cannot see.

Now it is night. I have locked her in this pyramid
of my own free will. She toys with the unwinding
sheet of a mummified king, paws at royal jewels
and sighs.
As I sleep at the 5 a.m. poem's edge she sniffs my skin
for news of her old lost world.

She names the Princes as they pass
heading for Bay Street in the winter blight.

They are always projecting themselves.
This is confidential.

Now it is morning in North Nineteen Hundred and Eighty.
The message clear: price of gold slumps,
war cracks at the border.
The Queen's cold mouth sends warning:

Beware.

How to get out of the poem without a scratch?
Each cast of the line seductive and minimal.
The ramp of the poem folding against
the power of the cat.
Possible use: to hold the bones of little ones
who cannot speak for themselves
or the Goddess Bastet.

Possible worth: treasure beyond speech
out of the old tomb, out of the mind's
sarcophagus. Wanting to touch
wanting to stare at her agate eyes
in the dark night of a museum postcard.

Bastet!
She moves toward me. She is here –
HISS HISS
With one paw raised
she scratches the final hieroglyphs
at the end of a bronze poem
I cannot see.

Gwendolyn MacEwen 1941-1987

Gwen, I didn't know it had been so bad, such a long way
down these past months to the *Afterworlds*, or that the
door and the blue wings opened and closed in that sound
of death you said you knew the tune of. Your last poems
so big with cosmos & semen & gold – and I'm afraid
adjectives that came too easily over the years: *terrible,
beautiful, splendid, fabulous, wonderful, remarkable,
dark, exquisite, mighty* – all of which you were as your
cat waited to take over the typewriter and get on with its
sublime works while you were out colliding with Barker
Fairley in a metaphysical blizzard or handing a coin to
the ferryman for the last ride.

*The Loneliness of the Long Distance Poet. Red Curtains.
The White Horse. Late Song. A Stillness of Waiting. The
Death of the Loch Ness Monster in the vast spaces of
the subatomic world where Matter has a   tendency
to exist ... Here where events have a   tendency   to
occur ...*

As you lay there dying in seizure was it your lord Life or
your lord Death who came to collect a last poem as you
careened into *the beautiful darkness*? And was it really
beautiful? Tell me. Was it dark? Or did the cat get your
last fabulous word?

Cue Cards

Fabulous fold of the gray cloud
over the banked white one –

Stolen thunder. Stolen gold.

Heart of the jungle darkness.
Hot death. Rousseau and Conrad

meet at the river bank
stare at their outstretched hands

that hold no clues.
Clueless. Monsieur Rousseau

falls down in a faint
seeing stars and shepherdesses.

And Mr. Conrad stumbles on
lured by drumbeats.

Half dead at the end of
his story, he leaves his trail –

and another Rousseau, Henri,
paints stripes on a large cat

as it royally passes through customs.

'Diplomatic Pouch'

Alfred Hitchcock steers his stomach across
the screen, a pregnant pause in the action,
the pit of wit. A note passes from hand
to hand, a message on form and function;
female fear splits the bathroom tiles,
'improved binoculars', 'Pain fountain'.
The romantic couple cast long glances
and smoke from their silver lair; birds
zoom down like missiles, testing, testing?

I loved the sophistication of every move,
sly camera angles, clues and accents, that
touch of class. And the neurotic gloss
on the whole murderous enterprise, the old
master's nasty mind that took us for
what we were worth.

'Thinking Cap'

The red hat
sails
through a rift
in my skull
out and over the
waiting audience
it's the colour of
red peppers
it's a flying
saucer
hovering there
spying and spritely
elvish in the coy
mood of not being
a red wheel
barrow
as mute though
as silent-speaking
this thing / spinning
over your head
preparing to land
fasten your seatbelt
lady and don't smoke

we're coming in
to Williamsland
to invade
the objects
to snatch the
after-image of
ol' Bill's plums –
you know –
the ones that
tasted so good
because they were
cold and beautiful
and couldn't

speak

'Cat & Mouse Game'

The cat steps over
    the rules of the game
      he, she, it crosses

the green playing field
    this is where I lie down
      to smell the daisies.

Mouse comes out of her house
    doing everything wrong
      thinks I'm a sunny day

which I think so too
    sprawled here pondering
      law and order.

J'accuse, j'accuse,
    j'accuse!
      Have I struck

the right note?
    I exit the scene
      paring my fingernails.

The field surges behind me
    with fun & names
      disrupting the bloody text.

Performance

Who is this *I* infesting my poems? Is it I hiding behind the Trump type on the page of the book you are reading? Is it a photograph of me on the cover of *Wilson's Bowl*? Is it I? *I* said, *I* say, *I* am saying –

I am the mask, the voice, the one who begins those lyrical poems, *I wandered lonely as a cloud ... I hear the Shadowy Horses, their long manes a-shake ... I am of Ireland / And the Holy Land of Ireland ... I, the poet William Yeats ... I am worn out with dreams ...*

Or am I reading, as they say, 'in person', in the first person? I step up to the microphone. I wait for you to cough with my damaged lungs. *'I am with you.'* The poem ends. I move into my higher consciousness, my lower voice, my sense of the present, my invocation, my prayer, my tiny faith in the typewritten words before me. The poem begins.

Listen: Do you hear the *I* running away with the man in the green hat? Look again. *I* is off and diving into Fulford Harbour to run with the whales. *I* spout. *I* make whalesong. Passengers on the ferry swarm to starboard to see me disporting myself. *I / we* know they are out to get us. Yes, they are mad for education. They'll pen us up at Sealand and we'll die. We don't build big and we can't shoot. *I* commits suicide in the watery commune, the vocal pod. *We* swims on.

I am performing this poem thinking of bill bissett at whose last performance he did not perform. He put on a record and left the room. 'Wow', as bill would say. But the whales have made it through Active Pass. They pass on the message: *Put on the record.* Sonar pulses ring for miles. Paul Horn is in the Temple of Heaven playing flute ... *Put on the record.*

I devise. You devise. We devise. To be together briefly with the page, the fallen timber. Or with me here standing before you wondering if the mike is on, if my mask is on, *persona,* wondering what to read next, or whether you'll turn the page. Like the state, I do not wither away, though the end is near.

I enter the Edge of Night. I join the cast of General Hospital. *I hear the Shadowy Horses, their long manes a-shake* ... I am only a partial fiction. *Look.* I hand you a golden jonquil. *Here. Now. Always.* On the outgoing breath of the whales.

Paradise Island

The woman takes the ferry to Salt Spring Island, proceeds to the local Pharmasave, which is ablaze with irrelevance and consumer goods. It's where we all come to. Pharmaceuticals and sleaze, catfood, toilet paper, makeup, deodorants, sweat-shirts, stationery, chocolate bars, soap, et cetera. This is Paradise, the tourist brochures and I say so. Hundreds of acres of trees are being clear-cut today, here, right now, to produce the paper to advertise the sleaze, vitamin pills, corn removers, hair removers, cleansing creams, biscuits, jujubes, hairclips, fingernail polish, earrings, scissors, toothpaste, Timex watches. She walks the long aisle and aims for the pharmacist. She demands 100 seconal and 100 dollars, and says she has a gun, which she hasn't. The pharmacist counts out 100 pills and five twenties. She ups the ante – another hundred. He counts again and when her hands are full he grabs her, and the RCMP arrive. It's Saturday.

Spring is already here in Ganges, in Paradise. Easter cards, chocolate bunnies, spring-coloured eggs, yellow ribbon for wrapping gifts. The resurrection. Condoms, jellies, foams, pills, magazines selling sex and beautiful B.C.

The woman from the mainland, of no fixed address, is removed to Victoria, a little bit of Olde England. And then it's Monday. She's 39 and she's suicidal. They'll keep her in jail until a doctor comes – perhaps on Wednesday.

This story is taking far too long to tell, but this is an exceptional event for the local Pharmasave. What a Saturday, they say, as it turns into legend, and right after *that* another woman comes in and we catch her shoplifting! But what did she lift: toothbrush, tampax, iron pills, flea collar, vaginal spray, videotapes, alarm clock, perfume, shampoo, peroxide, garbage bags? The mythological proportions of the story are splendid, if obvious. Eve, the first woman to be seduced by advertising and deathwish, is at it again, agog with superabundance and enclosure, slightly west-south and light years east of Eden.

Bronwen's Earrings

long, or large and circular
the only decoration on her
tall frame, her plain façade
the better to hear the high
vibrations of your health, your
sorrows. A touch of fantastic
as she moved her head
to follow the plot
silver or gold flashing
hilarious light on the lure
of the pierced ear.
Spangles. Trapezoids, fluttery
things. Wild bird.

The pair I gave her
turquoise, oval, Chinese
I think and very long
with a history of survival.

As I drink this tea
on an ordinary day
someone crosses
a street in Kingston
picking up flute notes
soprano complaints
her earlobes tugged
by a small weight
of chimes
the need to be heard, desire.

The Making of a Japanese Print

The first plate in the volume is the key block
giving the outline. It is easy to see how each
successive color is added by a separate block to
achieve the final result.
from The Making of a Japanese Print

Imprint No. 1

Eye contact, and it's forever.
The first circle.

And then the breast
the left or right.
So choice.
Or grab what is given.

Rosebud and at the
periphery / eyelash
dark sandals pass by.

Add a chair in the corner
with a white chemise.
This is the only way to go
– outward.

Door behind the mother
closing as father in blue
blows out.

White filled in, hatch-
crossings for negative space.
Decadent life.

Flesh tint laid on
with extreme caution.
All moves are dangerous:

open the door and wind pours in
with dust. Lift the head
of mother an inch
her attention goes
out the unseen window.

If baby sleeps
hand falling away from
the opening bud, rose
becomes dream, memory
a praise of distance.

*Technique is all
a test of the artist's
sincerity.* Oh
we are *sincere,* we go
for the blade, cut close
to the bone. The splotch
of red in the lower right-hand
corner, a sign of the happy
maker.

Imprint No. 2

Knife. Chisel. Mallet.
Block of cherry wood.
Printing pad. Paper. Ink.

What does he think?

He floats a green
into the space
of its assignation.
A world divides
the view from an empty
chair shifts

a chair with a life of its own
an orange cushion.
Poppies arise from extinction
on the plane of the sun.

Harunobu, your hand trembles.
You will die young and lucky.
Sit down in the chair you
yourself have provided.
The curved form is a fan
alarmingly pink.
Flutter the air.

Intaglio for what you see best
the 'empty imprint'?
What you see best
is the ivory kimono
coming towards you.
It will stay in the same place
always, Harunobu, brocading
the threat of advance.

A mere press of your hands
and your death flies
into a silken shadow.

Then washy blue three-quarters up.

Imprint No. 3

A fake. There was no chair
no washy blue in the 'Heron Maid'.
I made it up for my own artistic
purposes. I was thinking of
Van Gogh, of myself sitting down
for the last time and getting
up again to make this confession.

Tree, shrubs, a turquoise stream
a Japanese woman dressed for cold
her parasol a shield against the
snow which we can't see falling.
One ear pokes out, too high up
from under her brown hood
yet all is harmonious.

In the floating world
she stands quite still
like the snowy heron
who is really always moving.
She is also winter and tells me
more about herself than Harunobu
wanted me to know.

Imprint No. 4

The Heron Maid steps
on her wooden blocks
off the path
into summer.
She removes her winter
cloak, her sandals
dips her feet
in the turquoise stream.
What does she think
as she sits on the verge
this side of anonymous water?
She uncoils her hair
slips off her rings
imagines a different future.
She thinks of Harunobu
working away at his
butcher blocks
his famous seasons.

She'll have to change
habits and colors
wash off her fear.
Perhaps she'll look
for another job
cut her hair short
change her expression.
And, it's possible, die
some day in foreign arms
under the new dispensation.

Each block is laid on
with extreme caution

then set aside
out of harm's way.

A woman emerges at last
on the finest paper, cursing
his quest for the line
and this damned delicate fan
carved in her hand
to keep her forever cool
factitious, apparently pleasing.

Phyllis Webb lives on Salt Spring Island, B.C. In the eighties she published *Wilson's Bowl*, *Talking* (essays), *Sunday Water*, *The Vision Tree* (Governor General's Award for Poetry, 1982), and *Water and Light*. *Hanging Fire* is her eleventh collection of poetry.

Editor for the Press:
Christopher Dewdney

Cover Design: Shari Spier / Reactor
Cover Photo: Michael Ondaatje
Text Design: Nelson Adams
Author Photo: Sonja A. Skarstedt
Typeset in Trump and printed in Canada

Coach House Press
401 (rear) Huron Street
Toronto, Canada M5S 2G5